HAMSA DESIGNS
COLORING BOOK

Mary Agredo
and
Javier Agredo

Dover Publications, Inc.
Mineola, New York

Note

The popular, palm-shaped *Hamsa*, usually seen wall hangings, art, and jewelry, is generally considered to be a sign of protection, courage, and good luck. Although the earliest evidence of the symbol has been dated back to ancient Mesopotamia, today the *Hamsa* is usually associated with several modern day religions. In Islam, it is known as the *Hand of Fatima*, representative of Muhammed's daughter, Fatima Zahra; Christians refer to it as the *Hand of Mary*, evocative of the Virgin Mary; and in Judaism it is believed that the five fingers represent the five senses which should be used to praise God. In all cases, the *Hamsa* is almost exclusively portrayed as art, often intricately carved or painted, thus making it an ideal selection for a coloring motif. This coloring book, part of Dover Publications' *Creative Haven* series, was designed with the experienced colorist in mind. Each plate contains a highly detailed illustration of the *Hamsa* set against decorative backgrounds and borders, perfect for experimenting with color, technique, or media. Plus, the perforated pages make displaying your finished work easy.

Bibliographical Note

Hamsa Designs Coloring Book is a new work, first published by
Dover Publications, Inc., in 2014.

International Standard Book Number

ISBN-13: 978-0-486-49454-8
ISBN-10: 0-486-49454-3

Manufactured in the United States by Courier Corporation
49454301   2014
www.doverpublications.com

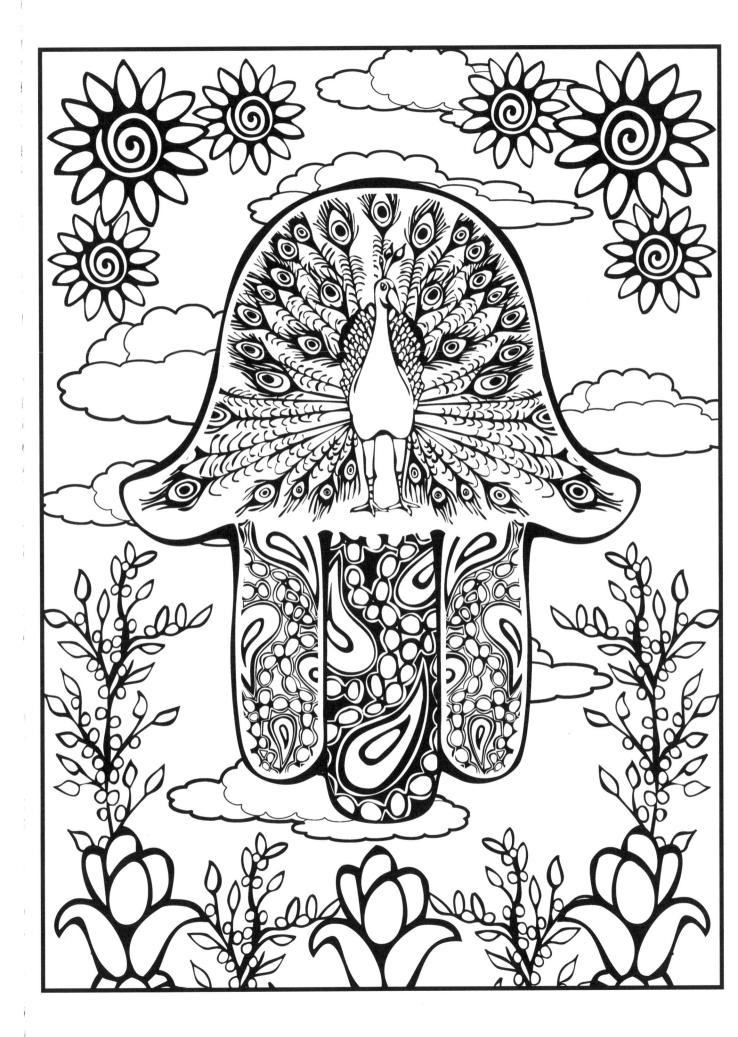